Talkin' Union:

The American Labor Movement

edited and introduced by
Juliet Haines Mofford

*The story of the labor movement needs to be taught in
every school in this land....America is a living testimonial
to what free men and women organized in free and
democratic trade unions can do to make a better life....
We ought to be proud of it.*

— U. S. Senator Hubert H. Humphrey
Democrat-Minnesota, 1977

Discovery Enterprises, Ltd.
Carlisle, Massachusetts

© Discovery Enterprises, Ltd., Carlisle, MA 1997

ISBN 1-878668-79-X paperback edition
Library of Congress Catalog Card Number 96-84729

10   9   8   7   6   5   4   3   2   1

Printed in the United States of America

Subject Reference Guide:

Talkin' Union: The American Labor Movement
edited and introduced by Juliet Haines Mofford

Labor Movement — U. S. History

Unions — U. S. History

Strikes — U. S. History

Labor Reform — U. S. History

Photos/Illustrations:

Cover illustration: Industrial Workers of the World poster

Other photos and illustrations are credited
where they appear in the book.

Table of Contents

Foreword 5
   Solidarity Forever 6

Farm to Factory to Organized Labor 9
   Shoeless Philly 10
   Workingmen's Parties 10
   The Lowell Female Labor Reform Association 11
   Lynn Shoeworkers Turn Out 12
   National Trade Labor Union 12
   Abraham Lincoln's Views on Labor 13

Talkin' Union 14
   A Giant Brotherhood of Toil — Knights of Labor 14
   "The Great Upheaval" — The Railway Strike of 1877 15
   The American Federation of Labor 16
   Samuel Gompers' Views on Strikes 18
   Who Threw the Bomb in Haymarket Square? 19
   Lock-Out! The Homestead Battle 22
   Eugene V. Debs (1855-1926) 24
   The Pullman Strike 25
   Trust-Busters 27
   TR Takes Charge 28

Out of the Sweatshops 29
   The Cost of a $5 Dress 29
   When Workers Were "Sweaters" 30
   Uprising of the 20,000 32
   Rules for Pickets 34
   Tragedy at Triangle 35
   Not in Vain 36
   Bread and Roses 38
   The Lawrence Textile Strike 39
   Recollections of a Young Worker 40
   Elizabeth Gurley Flynn: The Rebel Girl 43

Birth of the Department of Labor 46
   The Clayton Act 47
   The Great Steel Strike 48
   The New Deal — Labor's Golden Years 49

John L. Lewis: The Miners' Friend 51
John L. Lewis Organizes the Unorganized! 51
Strikers, Sit Down! 53
The Taft-Hartley Act 55

New Strength in the 20th Century 57
Labor Finds Strength in Unity — AFL-CIO 57
La Huelga! and the California Grape Boycott 59
La Causa 60
President Kennedy's Tribute to Unions 62

Suggested Further Reading 63

Teaching Aids, Songs, Graphics, and Videos 64

About the Editor 64

Foreword

If the workers took a notion, They could stop all speeding trains;
Every ship upon the ocean, They could tie with mighty chains.
Every wheel in the creation, Every mine and every mill;
Fleets and armies of the nation,
Will, at the workers' command stand still.

— Joe Hill

The history of the American labor movement is the story of millions of working people joining together to rally for a common cause. It has been a long, hard, and sometimes violent struggle, as workers fought abuses and demanded social justice and human dignity. The history of organized labor is about people in a democratic society with common needs, cooperating for progress and protection. One worker, unable to provide for his or her family on meager wages, was helpless against a powerful employer. Organizing with other workers who had the same problems, he or she stood a better chance of bringing about change. Throughout history, workers have united in craft guilds, workingmen's parties, and unions to win rights they could never have gotten alone.

Labor unions have given workers a political voice in key issues that affect their lives. Before unions, there were no laws to protect workers; no rules for employers regarding safe workplaces; no limit to the number of hours a boss could demand from his workforce. Before unions, workers did not dare complain for fear of losing their jobs. Just to win the right to organize and gain recognition has been difficult.

Many of the benefits we take for granted today were won for us over generations by organized labor. Before unions, Americans did not even have free public education. Minimum wage laws, number of hours in a work day, rules against child labor, health care, medical assistance for senior citizens, disability compensation, unemployment benefits, paid holidays, severance pay, and social security have all been won by union representatives who lobbied, legislated, fought, and even died to obtain these rights now guaranteed all Americans by law.

The history of the labor movement is about how working people and their unions achieved these rights which have improved the quality of our lives.

Songs have been an important part of the American labor movement since its beginning. Singing raised workers' spirits during difficult times, and helped unify them as they struggled and marched to achieve common goals and realize hopes for a better life. Of hundreds of union songs, this one is perhaps the most familiar. It was written in 1915 by Ralph Chaplin for the Industrial Workers of the World (IWW) and sung to the Civil War tune *John Brown's Body* or *Battle Hymn of the Republic.*

Solidarity Forever

When the union's inspiration through the workers' blood shall run,
There can be no power greater anywhere beneath the sun;
Yet no force on earth is weaker than the feeble strength of one,
But the union makes us strong.

CHORUS: Solidarity forever!
Solidarity forever!
Solidarity forever!
For the union makes us strong!

They have taken untold millions that they never toiled to earn,
But without our brain and muscle not a single wheel could turn.
We can break their haughty power, gain our freedom when we learn
That the union makes us strong.

In our hands is placed the power greater than their hoarded gold,
Greater than the might of armies magnified a hundred fold.
We can bring to birth a new world from the ashes of the old,
For the union makes us strong.

— Ralph Chaplin

Throughout history, labor and management have often been in disagreement. The worker consistently wants a fair wage for a day's work, while the manager seeks the highest possible profit. Unions take the workers' side and strive for *conflict resolution.* A shop usually has a representative elected by union members to oversee daily conditions at the workplace. He reports *grievances* to the local union chapter, which is where members also pay union dues (often used to support workers' families during strikes).

Locals belong to area associations, where members meet to share common concerns and complaints. A national union organization like AFL-CIO establishes union rules and lobbies legislators to bring about laws for social and economic change that will benefit workers.

By filing grievances through the union, workers are usually able to keep their jobs while trying to improve working conditions. If management and union representatives are unable to come to any agreement through *collective bargaining*, a third party may be called in to participate in settling the dispute by listening to both sides in an effort to bring about compromise and settlement of grievances. When the third party does not have the authority to determine the outcome, he or she is called a *mediator.* When the third party is authorized to bind the parties to some outcome, he or she is called an *arbitrator.*

A *strike* is a last resort and is only called when all other negotiations have failed or management refuses to recognize the union or meet with grievance committees. Workers seldom want to go out on strike because during a strike they give up their paychecks, often lose their jobs, and sometimes even lose their lives.

Mill and mine owners used certain tactics in order to control their workers and break strikes without granting labor's demands. They put signs around the factory to threaten the jobs of employees who might be tempted to complain about working overtime: "If you can't come in on Sunday, don't come in on Monday!" If a strike has been called, a manager might call a *lockout* and shut down his factory so workers do not get paid. Managers often hired private detectives as industrial spies to join unions and report back to them with the names of labor organizers, who would then be fired and *blacklisted*, so they wouldn't get hired anywhere else. *Strike breakers*, or *scabs*, were hired to break picket lines and replace striking workers at their jobs. An employer might require his employees to sign *yellow-dog contracts*, agreeing not to join a union. Some managers declared their companies *open shops*, meaning that no one belonging to a union would be hired there.

Some people think only of strikes when they think of labor unions. Many labor leaders did not even believe in strikes, which they thought turned public opinion against labor. Some Americans still believe that professional workers, such as nurses and teachers, should not be allowed to form unions or to strike.

Calvin Coolidge was Governor of Massachusetts in 1919 when 1,544 Boston police walked off their beats after the Commissioner suspended them for joining a union. Coolidge became a national hero after proclaiming: "There is no right to strike against the public safety by anybody, anywhere, anytime!" He sent in several thousand state militiamen, then asked the U.S. secretary of war for federal troops. Many Americans agreed with Coolidge that it was the policemen's "patriotic duty" to go back to work.

Only selected landmarks from labor's long and complicated history and the ideas of some of the movement's most significant leaders are presented here. How did unions get started and why are they still important to American democracy? Why is the history of the American labor movement marked by conflict and, often, violence? What points of view did various American presidents express regarding labor, and what role has government played in labor history? What changes in U.S. law have made a significant difference in the lives of working people?

It is impossible to include all the struggles workers faced as they fought for equal pay for equal work, a fair day's wage, and safety and health in the workplace. There are tragedies as well as great achievements in labor's long and courageous struggle to attain a decent life for all working people. Labor's challenges continue as unions strive to preserve those rights already won and to meet new challenges facing working people today.

Farm to Factory to Organized Labor

*To be independent for the comforts of life, we must make them ourselves....
Manufacturers are now as necessary to our independence as to our Comfort....We
must now place the manufacturer by the side of the agriculturalist.*

— Thomas Jefferson, 1816

At the time Thomas Jefferson wrote the Declaration of Independence, he
hoped that the future of the new nation would be based upon agriculture.
He said he "never wished to see citizens occupied at workbenches." Yet the
Revolutionary War, trade embargoes, European wars, and the War of 1812
made it clear that this country could no longer depend on foreign imports.

The Industrial Revolution changed the nature of work itself. The new
textile machinery produced cloth three times faster than a colonial woman
could twist yarn at her spinning wheel or a journeyman weaver could create
on his loom. Improved methods of transportation, new highways and bridges,
the canal system, steamboats, and soon, railways, meant wider availability
of raw materials and access to growing markets.

It was difficult for a worker to feel that same sense of pride when he no
longer made an entire product, but had become only a part of the process,
repeating the same task over and over again at a machine. Days and duties
were now governed by the clock. Managers seldom considered the health of
employees, put money into improving factory safety, or cared that workers'
wages were too low to support families. Owners and stockholders reaped
huge profits and frequently speeded-up machines, set clocks back, and
assigned workers more machines to operate, all without raising wages. Whenever there was an economic depression, managers would cut wages or lay
off part of the workforce. There was no *unemployment compensation* to
tide fired workers over while they looked for other jobs. Anyone who complained risked getting *blacklisted.* Workers could be easily replaced by the
increasing number of immigrants flooding into America, or by women and
children willing to work for lower wages.

Workers soon realized they could accomplish more by joining together
in a common effort to improve their lives. First, there were local trade unions,
organized by occupations, which usually disbanded after immediate aims were
achieved. In 1786, for example, New York printers formed the Typographical
Society and went on strike demanding wages be increased to $1 a day.

Shoeless Philly

The new factories could turn out a hundred shoes to every pair created by a cobbler's hands. Shoes made-to-order with awl and peg still fit better, so cordwainers (as shoemakers were called after the quality leather that came from Cordoba, Spain) erected *ten-by-tens*, small shoe shops in every town. Yet no matter how hard they worked, there was no way they could keep up with market demands. Shoe prices dropped so low that workers couldn't feed their families. When the shoemakers of Philadelphia went on strike, a court found them "guilty of conspiracy to restrain American trade."

The Federal Society of Journeymen Cordwainers of Philadelphia, formed in 1792, is considered the first actual union. No shoes or boots were made in Philadelphia in 1799 during its 10-week strike for a 10-hour day, higher wages, and better working conditions. In 1806, eight union members went to jail on charges of *criminal conspiracy* for forming a labor organization, and trade unions became illegal.

Workingmen's Parties

Workingmen's Parties became common during Andrew Jackson's presidency. The first political party sponsored by labor was the Workingman's Party founded about 1828 by the Journeymen Carpenters of Philadelphia. Members of the Mechanics Union of Trade Associations voted to nominate candidates for the state and national legislature who would support workers. They helped get Andrew Jackson elected president in 1828 and 1832. However, Jackson became the first presidential strikebreaker in 1834, when he sent federal troops to crush a strike of Irish workers on the Chesapeake and Ohio Canal.

The first national federation of labor unions was formed in New York in 1834. Women and free blacks were excluded from membership. At this time, when employers could keep workers on the job from dawn to dusk, strikes to shorten hours swept the country. By 1860, seven states had made the 10-hour workday law. The National Trades' Union dissolved during the economic depression of 1837-1839, which caused many factories to close and businesses to fail, leaving one-third unemployed.

In 1842, seven Journeymen Bootmakers Society of Boston members went on trial before the Massachusetts Supreme Court for "unlawfully and deceitfully" uniting into an illegal society (*Commonwealth v. Hunt*). Chief Justice Lemuel Shaw dismissed charges of criminal conspiracy and decreed it no longer illegal to establish unions or for workers to join an organization for protection of their trades. Shaw also ruled it legal to strike.

The Lowell Female Labor Reform Association

President Andrew Jackson was among the many visitors to praise the new industrial city of Lowell. The Lowell Experiment was widely acclaimed, particularly for its well-disciplined workforce, chiefly made up of the daughters of New England farmers, who worked at spinning frames and power looms 12-14 hours a day, six days a week for $3.50 or less.

The Lowell Female Labor Reform Association was organized in 1844 under the leadership of mill girl and militant labor reformer Sarah Bagley, who campaigned for a shorter workday. Although women would not gain the right to vote for another seventy-six years, they could influence government through petitions.

Although its first petition to the Massachusetts Legislature was denied, the LFLRA joined with the New England Workingmen's Association to try again, and Massachusetts became the first state to seriously consider the health and safety of its factory workers.

Source: *Voice of Industry*, Lowell, MA. January 15, 1845.

We the undersigned, peaceable, industrious and hard-working men and women of Lowell, in view of our condition...toiling from 13 to 14 hours per day, confined in unhealthy apartments, exposed to the poisonous contagion of air, vegetable, animal, and mineral properties, debarred from proper Physical Exercise, time for Mental Discipline and Mastication cruelly limited; and thereby hastening us on through pain, disease and privation, down to a premature grave, pray the legislature to institute a ten hour working day in all of the factories of the state.

Signed: John Quincy Adams Thayer,
Sarah G. Bagley, James Carle, and 2000 others.

Sarah Bagley was blacklisted as a troublemaker. Many mill girls were soon comparing their lot with that of black slaves in the South. As Yankee farm girls left the factories, they were replaced by immigrants, glad to find any job.

Lynn Shoeworkers Turn Out

American Ladies will not be slaves!
Give us a fair compensation and we will labor cheerfully! -- A Lynn striker

In 1860, the largest strike, or *turn out* as it was then called, occurred in Lynn, Massachusetts when 5,000 men and 1,000 women shoe workers left their jobs and paraded through the streets. After two months, the strikers won their wage increase.

The public thought women who worked for wages were abandoning their true roles as wives and mothers. Nineteenth century women had no political voice and had a hard time getting recognized by organized labor. Yet as early as 1831, 1,600 tailoresses went on strike in New York, following a series of wage cuts.

The first union to admit women was the Cigarmakers' Union in 1867. Some male workers believed wages were kept down because women were willing to work for less. Others said that women who worked were taking jobs away from the men. The American Federation of Labor excluded women workers for many years, believing that men's wages should be high enough so that women would not have to go out to work.

National Trade Labor Union

We are all one family of slaves together.
The labor movement is a second Emancipation Proclamation!

— William H. Sylvis, NTLU Convention, 1866

William H. Sylvis, America's first great labor leader, was an iron molder from Pennsylvania, who had organized fifty-three local craft unions into the Iron Molders International Union. In August of 1866, seventy-seven trade union delegates representing 60,000 workers from thirteen states met in Baltimore to found the first National Labor Congress ever convened in the United States. By 1868, this was known as the National Trade Labor Union (NTLU). It became the first labor organization with political influence, when it got a law through Congress legally establishing the eight hour work day for mechanics and laborers employed by the federal government.

By 1872, NTLU had become the National Reform and Labor Party and was dedicated to arbitration and political action. Although it did not survive long past the "Panic of 1873," with its national economic collapse and three million unemployed, it laid the foundations for future unions.

Abraham Lincoln's Views on Labor

Lincoln's 1860 campaign slogan was *Free Soil, Free Speech, Free Labor,* and *Free Men!* Because Lincoln was sympathetic to early organized labor, his candidacy was generally supported by the nation's workers, no matter how they felt about the slavery issue.

Source: William Cahn. *Speeches of Abraham Lincoln, Pictorial History of American Labor: The Contributions of the Working Men & Women to America's Growth, from Colonial Times to the Present.* New York: Crown, 1972, pp. 89-90.

All that serves labor serves the nation....

The strongest bond of human sympathy, outside of the family relation, should be one uniting all working people of all nations, and tongues, and kindreds....

Thank God we have a system of labor where there can be a strike. Whatever the pressure, there is a point where the working man may stop....

— Hartford, Connecticut, March 5, 1860

All that harms labor is treason to America. No line can be drawn between these two. If any man tells you he loves America, yet he hates labor, he is a liar. If a man tells you he trusts America, yet fears labor, he is a fool.

— Lincoln's Reply to Committee of New York Workingmen's Association, March 21, 1864

America changed dramatically in the decades following the Civil War. The nation became an industrial power on the world scene and millions of workers were needed to mine coal for fuel and steam power, shape steel to make bridges, trains, ships, and machinery, build the railroads, and operate factory machines.

The faster products could be manufactured, the higher the profits that came to those who owned the mines and mills. Eli Whitney is credited with developing mass production techniques, in 1798, that were to change the way things were made. Elias Howes' sewing machine of 1846 gradually moved clothing production into the factories. In the 1850s, Isaac Singer used assembly lines to make his sewing machines. Things now produced piece-by-piece on machines operated by unskilled workers spelled the end of the traditional American crafts person.

Talkin' Union

A Giant Brotherhood of Toil — Knights of Labor

Storm the fort, ye Knights of Labor
Battle for your cause;
Equal rights for every neighbor
Down with tyrant laws.

Toiling millions now are waking
See them marching on.
All the tyrants now are shaking,
Ere their power is gone.

A Philadelphia tailor named Uriah Stephens dreamed of a great brotherhood that would unite skilled and unskilled workers, so they could receive their fair share of the nation's wealth. His hope was that The Noble and Holy Order of the Knights of Labor would be *"A Giant Brotherhood of Toil"* and raise workers out of wage slavery, without strikes or boycotts.

When Stephens resigned in 1879, Terrence V. Powderly (1849-1924) replaced him as *"Grand Master Workman."* Powderly was a social reformer, in favor of abolishing the wage system for cooperatively owned shops. He did not believe that strikes proved a successful means of achieving aims and thought workers and employers should set up Boards of Arbitration instead.

The motto of The Order of the Knights of Labor, as Powderly renamed this society, was "An injury to one is the concern of all." Membership was open to all "men and women of every craft, creed and color." Under Powderly's leadership and until 1893, the Knights of Labor was the largest, most significant labor organization in the country. The Knights' greatest victory came in 1885 when shopmen at Jay Gould's Southwestern Railroads went on strike and got management to negotiate their grievances.

In the 1890s many Knights resigned to join the newly organized American Federation of Labor (AF of L). The Knights of Labor represented the forerunner of the trade unionism of the 1930s, when such industrial unions would be established by the Congress of Industrial Organizations (CIO).

"The Great Upheaval" — The Railway Strike of 1877

Leslie's Illustrated Newspaper, 1877. (LOC)

Armed strikers drag strikebreakers from a freight train.

American industry increasingly depended upon its national network of railways. Goods manufactured in eastern factories could easily be shipped to markets out west. Working on the railroad was dangerous. Derailings were common. Engineers often received injuries from flying sparks and scalding steam. Brakemen and switchmen lost fingers and legs or slipped beneath trains and lost their lives. There was no workmen's compensation nor any insurance or pension plan to support their widows and children.

The Great Railway Strike of 1877 marked the beginning of long labor unrest among the exploited railroad workers and their bosses. No union organized the country's first violent confrontation of labor and management on the railroads, which erupted in Martinsburg, West Virginia on July 16, over wage cuts and blacklisting for union membership by the Baltimore and Ohio Railroad Company. The strike, referred to in newspapers of that day as *The Great Upheaval*, spread to the Pennsylvania Railroad and soon, more than 100,000 railroad workers in fourteen states had walked off their jobs and were smashing railcars and pulling up tracks in Boston, Chicago, St. Louis, Toledo, Louisville, Buffalo, and San Francisco. When 1,000 state troopers arrived in Pittsburgh on July 21, citizens threw stones and the militia fired into the crowd, killing twenty and wounding thirty.

Taking the side of business, President Hayes ordered two hundred federal troops to Martinsburg to reopen the B & O rail lines. Before train service could be restored to the nation, more than a hundred were dead, hundreds injured, thousands jailed, and $5 million in railroad property had been destroyed. Workers returned to their jobs without a pay raise. The strike resulted in stricter laws against unions and the buildup of state militias.

The American Federation of Labor

Fair day's wage for fair day's work

" What does labor want?" Samuel Gompers was often asked by the press. "More and more, here and now! Wages, benefits, better and safer working conditions!" replied the President of the American Federation of Labor.

Source: Samuel Gompers, AFL Convention, Chicago, 1893.

We want more schoolhouses and less jails;
More books and less arsenals;
More learning and less vice;
More constant work
And less crime;
More leisure and less greed;
More justice and less revenge;
In fact, more of the opportunities to cultivate our better natures.

We are educating the public to the eight-hour movement; teaching America the evils of sweatshops, tenement factories, and child labor. That kind of education brings results.

It is not our purpose to bring the workers Beethoven and Shakespeare; it is our purpose to bring good food into their kitchens and clean toilets into their factories. When we have won the economic fight, the men will be free to pursue whatever life they want. Every hour spent in a filthy tenement factory, and every unfed child at mealtime is a crime against humanity....

For thirty-seven years, Samuel Gompers represented the single most important force in the American labor movement. He had immigrated from London at 13, the family's passage paid by his father's Union of British Cigar Makers. Like so many other Jewish immigrants, the Gompers family rolled cigars in a New York City tenement. When Samuel was seventeen, he joined the union at the shop where he worked and led a strike which got him blacklisted. He soon became president of the New York local of Cigar Makers' International and was active in the Federation of Organized Trades and Labor Unions, whose main goal was the eight hour workday. The FOTLU, founded in 1881, was replaced by the American Federation of Labor, which Gompers and Peter McGuire of the Brotherhood of Carpenters co-founded in Columbus, Ohio, where some twenty-five unions met on December 8, 1886. Their goal was "to organize small trade unions into a powerful national organization and to protect the skilled labor of America...and to sustain the standard of American workmanship and skill."

President of the American Federation of Labor from 1886 (except for one year) until his death in 1924, Samuel Gompers believed that separate unions of skilled craftsmen should be organized by their occupations under a national umbrella. He thought these should be governed as independent trade unions with their own officers, constitutions and rules to deal with employers, in the same way federal government presided over states. This was different from Powderly's plan of one single union for skilled and unskilled workers. Unskilled workers, blacks, and women were originally excluded from membership in the AF of L. The AF of L signed on half a million members its first year and, by 1902, had more than a million. Dues and membership fees enabled the AF of L to hire and train union organizers and to provide financial aid to members on strike or during lockouts.

Gompers believed the main purpose of unions to be economic. He was a practical man, willing to compromise. In his opinion, progress for the labor movement would come gradually, by working within the system. He thought gains for labor should be won by collective bargaining. He worked with government and business to achieve AF of L aims and disassociated the organization from socialists and radicals.

The AF of L continually fought for higher wages, compulsory education laws, an end to child labor for all under fourteen, safety and health at the workplace, and legal protection against cheap foreign labor. Gompers believed all workers had earned the right to a decent standard of living.

Samuel Gompers' Views on Strikes

Samuel Gompers (1850-1924)

Samuel Gompers considered strikes lawful means of protest, but thought they should be a last resort when all attempts at arbitration had failed. In his view, radical protest endangered workers and put public opinion against labor.

Source: Morris B. Schnapper, *American Labor: A Pictorial Social History,* Public Affairs Press, Washington, D.C.: 1972, p. 336.

While some may assert that the strike is a relic of barbarism, I answer that the strike is the most highly civilized method which the workers, (the wealth producers), have yet devised to protest against the wrong and injustice, and to demand the enforcement of the right.

The strike compels more attention and study into economic and social wrongs than all the essays that have been written....It establishes better relations between the contending parties than have heretofore existed; reconciles laborers and capitalists more effectually, and speeds the machinery for production to a greater extent; and gives impetus to meaningful progress.

I trust that the day will never come when the workers, the wealth producers of our country and our time, will surrender their right to strike....

Who Threw the Bomb in Haymarket Square?

Source: Richard O. Boyer and Herbert M. Morais, *Labor's Untold Story,* New York: United Electrical, Radio & Machine Workers of America, 1955, p. 88.

We mean to make things over   We want to feel the sunshine;
We're tired of toil for nought   We want to smell the flowers
But bare enough to live on;   We're sure that God has never willed it
An hour for thought.   We mean to have eight hours!

      We're summoning our forces from
      Shipyard, shop and mill:
      Eight hours for work, eight hours for rest,
      Eight hours for what we will!

The Haymarket bombing of May 4, 1886 put a stop to workers' dreams for the eight-hour day for some time. It also made the public fearful of organized labor, which now seemed violent and un-American.

Labor organizers had called for a national strike on the first of May if employers had not granted the eight-hour workday by then. Some 350,000 workers all over the country unified in this general strike, while employers attempted to mobilize the national guard and hire Pinkerton Detectives and deputize special police. Philadelphia's textile industry shut down entirely. The 40,000 strikers in Chicago represented trades as varied as carpenters, bakers, railroad freightmen, meat packers, and metal workers. On May 3, workers at McCormick Harvester Company gathered to listen to strike leader August Spies. There was a confrontation between workers and the strike-breakers hired to replace them and 200 policemen rushed in to break up the crowd. They fired on the strikers, killing four and wounding fifty.

Source: *Ibid.,* p. 96.

"Workingmen, arm yourselves and appear in full force!" August Spies, representing the International Working People's Association, called a protest rally. The following evening some 300 gathered in Chicago's Haymarket Square to hear speeches by Spies, Albert Parsons and Samuel Fielden. Fielden was just concluding his talk when 180 policemen suddenly appeared. "In the name of the people of the State of Illinois, I command this meeting immediately and peaceably to disperse."

"We are peaceable," Fielden assured the officer. Suddenly, there was an explosion. The police sergeant died instantly and sixty-six lay injured. The police fired into the crowd and, within minutes, Haymarket Square was littered with dead and wounded policemen and workers.

"Hang them first and try them later! All radicals must be punished!" Many Americans agreed with the newspapers. Fielden, Parsons, Spies and four others were arrested for inciting to violence, since there was no evidence as to who threw the bomb or who was firing shots in the darkness and confusion. The press said it made no difference whether or not those arrested had thrown the bomb. "They should hang for their political words and activities and if more such troublemakers were given to the hangman, so much the better!"

Parsons claimed that "the bomb-thrower had been hired by the industrialists who were intent upon bombing the eight-hour day out of American life." On November 11, 1887, Albert Parsons was hanged with August Spies, Adolph Fischer, and George Engel.

Source: August Spies' gallows speech, *ibid.*, p. 101.

There will come a time when our silence will be more powerful than the voices you strangle today....If you think by hanging us you can stamp out the labor movement...the movement from which the downtrodden millions, the millions who toil in want and misery, expect salvation—if this is your opinion, then hang us! Here you will tread upon a spark but there and there, behind you and in front of you, and everywhere, the flames will blaze up. It is a subterranean fire. You cannot put it out.

Although Samuel Gompers had pleaded clemency for the condemned, he did not wish the AF of L linked in the public mind with Haymarket. Gompers said:

The effect of that bomb was that it not only killed the policemen, but it killed our eight-hour movement for that year and for a few years just after. Notwithstanding, we had absolutely no connection with these people.

Everywhere, trade union leaders were being arrested for rioting and conspiracy. *Yellow-dog contracts* and the hiring of industrial spies became more common. And because the most accused at Haymarket had been German immigrants, an anti-foreign hysteria swept across America.

Source: John Swinton's Paper, New York, 1886.

The bomb was a godsend to the enemies of the labor movement. They have used it as an explosive against all the objects that the working people are bent on accomplishing and in defense of all the evils that capital is bent on maintaining.

In 1893, the new governor released the men still in prison and pardoned those who had been executed, on grounds that they had not received a fair trial. The true identity of the person who threw the bomb in Haymarket Square remains a mystery.

Illustration of Haymarket riots, from Harper's Weekly *for May 15, 1886*

Lock-out! The Homestead Battle

Source: Penny Colman. *Strike! The Bitter Struggle of American Workers from Colonial Times to the Present.* Brookfield, CT: Millbrook Press, 1995, p. 42.

We are asking one another, as we pass the time of day,
Why workingmen resort to arms to get their proper pay,
And why our labor unions should not be recognized,
Whilst the action of a syndicate must not be criticized.

Now, the troubles down at Homestead were brought about this way:
When a grasping corporation had the audacity to say,
"You must all renounce your union and forswear your liberty;
And we will give you the chance to live and die in slavery.

One of labor history's most violent confrontations took place July 6, 1892 at Homestead Steel Works along the banks of the Monongahela River. One of twelve steel plants in the Pittsburgh area owned by Carnegie Steel Company, Homestead employed some 3,800 workers, mostly immigrants from Eastern Europe. Carnegie preferred to hire non-union, foreign-born workers because they would settle for lower wages and seldom complained about living or working conditions.

Andrew Carnegie's own parents had immigrated from Scotland and he started working in a textile factory at the age of thirteen for $1.20 a week. Now he cleared $20 million a year. Although Carnegie gave generously to charity and is admired for endowments that helped establish public libraries, the workers at his own steel company averaged $100 a month.

It was dangerous work and if you got scalded or lost an arm in the furnace, there was no *workman's compensation*. Unskilled steelmen worked twelve hours a day, six or seven days a week with only Christmas and the Fourth of July off. They lived in company-owned houses clustered above the river, hardly worth the rents collected by the company. Although the Amalgamated Association of Iron, Steel, and Tin Workers was the most powerful union in America at this time, it only admitted skilled workers. This meant that the majority of Homestead steelworkers could not join, although they could get organizers like Hugh O'Donnell to fight for them. Andrew Carnegie and his manager, Henry Clay Frick, had no intention of allowing the union to interfere with the way they ran their plant. They reduced wages and declared Homestead non-union. The union attempted to negotiate new contracts for the workers, but Carnegie refused to listen. He instructed Frick to shut down the plant and fire everyone, then left for vacation in Europe.

Lock-out! By mid-June the plant was surrounded by a fence three miles long and twelve feet high, topped with barbed wire and searchlights. Fort Frick, the workers called it. Frick offered to hire back anyone who would negotiate a personal contract on company terms, but no one signed. Then he sent for three hundred agents from the Pinkerton National Detective Agency to "protect property" so he could hire strikebreakers and reopen. Heavily armed, they arrived in two barges, towed up river by a tugboat.

"Go back or we'll not answer for your lives!" the strikers called, pointing rifles and picking up fence posts for clubs.

"We are coming up that hill!" the Pinkertons yelled back. "And we don't want any trouble from you men!" As the first one left the barge, a striker threw himself across the gangplank. When the detective attempted to step over the man, he was shot in the leg. The Pinkertons immediately fired into the crowd on the riverbank. The battle lasted twelve hours.

"Enough of the killing. On what terms do you wish to capitulate?" strike leader Hugh O'Donnell called out. Then strikers threw oil on the river and set it afire and the agents raised the white flag of surrender, agreeing to put down their rifles in exchange for safe conduct. As they passed through the mob, which included strikers' wives and children, they were plummeted by stones and clubs. When that terrible day ended, nine strikers and seven detectives lay dead, with some sixty men on both sides wounded. A week later, 8,000 state militiamen arrived to declare Homestead under martial law.

The Homestead strike damaged relations between organized labor and management. It represented the last significant effort of steelworkers to fight for better conditions for the next quarter of a century. The Amalgamated Association of Steel, Iron and Tin Workers was banned from the U.S. Steel Corporation, with which Carnegie's company merged. U.S. Steel would not recognize any union until 1937.

When it was over, Henry Clay Frick telegrammed Andrew Carnegie in Europe: "Our victory now complete and most gratifying. Do not think we will ever have serious labor trouble again. We had to teach our employees a lesson and we have taught them one they will never forget."

Carnegie's reply: "Life worth living again. Congratulate all around! Ever your Pard."

Eugene V. Debs (1855-1926)

*The capitalists refer to you as mill hands, farm hands, factory hands...
hands...hands...hands. A capitalist would feel insulted if you called him a
hand. He's a head. The trouble is he owns your head and your hands!*

— Eugene V. Debs, Brotherhood of Railroad Trainmen

Eugene Debs believed that only by organizing workers nationally by occupation could they could gain power and fair treatment. In 1893, in Chicago, hub of the nation's rail system, Debs founded the American Railway Union (ARU) which, unlike the AF of L, included both skilled and unskilled workers and was an industrial union. As president of the new ARU, Debs led a successful strike against the Great Northern Railway, which had cut wages three times in 1894. Railroaders won a pay raise and kept their jobs. This marked the first victory for any railroad union and made Debs the workers' hero.

Leader of the American Socialist Party, Debs ran for president of the United States five times between 1900 and 1920. He once ran from an Atlanta jail cell where, although serving time for opposition to America's entrance into World War I, he received over a million votes.

Posters that carried IWW slogans
Library of Congress

The Pullman Strike

George Mortimer Pullman made a fortune on his sleeping cars. Pullman cars were as lavish as the finest hotel lobbies of the period with velvet drapes, ornately carved interiors, and decorative furnishings. The finest chefs were hired to prepare elegant meals in plush dining cars. When the traveler was ready to retire, porters would unhinge upper and lower berths and make up cozy beds. Most Pullman porters were freed slaves and trained as *Ambassadors of Hospitality*. Because he offered jobs to so many ex-slaves, Frederick Douglass had once called George Pullman "the black workers' best friend." Yet no black workers were permitted to reside in Mr. Pullman's model town.

In 1881, Pullman developed a planned community outside Chicago, where his Pullman Palace Car Company was located. He established schools, parks, stores, and churches for his employees and their families. Everything was owned and regulated by the company. Living expenses, including rent, water and gas, even church fees, were deducted from railroaders' paychecks. Newspapers called it a "workers' paradise" and one of the "wonders of the west," but workers felt they were treated like medieval serfs.

Source: Boyer and Morais, *op. cit.*, pp. 124-29.

> We are born in a Pullman House, fed from the Pullman Shop, taught in the Pullman School, catechized in the Pullman Church, and when we die we shall be buried in the Pullman Cemetery and go to Pullman Hell.

The nation suffered a severe depression in 1893. Fewer Americans could afford to travel, so Pullman production was scaled down and half the workforce laid off. The rest received their fifth wage cut in a year, even though their rent remained the same. This meant that workers would be forced into debt to the company just to meet living costs. ARU members formed a Grievance Committee to get their wages restored and met with George Pullman, who offered to show them company ledgers to prove that falling sales made the reduction of wages necessary. He said he expected loyalty from all employees since he had "done so much for their well-being." Not only did Pullman refuse to restore wages or reduce rents, he fired the members of this committee the next day. On May 11, nearly 3,000 workers walked off their jobs and Mr. Pullman locked his plant, announcing that he "could wait until the men were hungry enough to go back to work." When Eugene Debs arrived in Pullman three days later, he found many workers in the company town near starvation. Debs urged arbitration, hoping to avoid any strike that might provoke violence, but Pullman management still refused to meet with union representatives.

The ARU voted to support the strike and to refuse to work on any trains with Pullman cars if the company did not arbitrate by June 26. No response was received from George Pullman so Debs called for a national boycott and ordered Pullman cars unhitched from all trains.

Source: Eugene V. Debs, ARU at Pullman, Ill., June, 1894. From Boyer and Morais, *op. cit.*, p. 125.

If it is a fact that after working for George M. Pullman for years you appear two weeks after your work stops, ragged and hungry, it only emphasizes the charge I made before this community, and Pullman stands before you a self-confessed robber. The paternalism of Pullman is the same as the self-interest of a slave-holder in his human chattels. You are striking to avert slavery and degradation.

The General Managers Association, which represented twenty-four railroads, was anxious to use this strike to destroy the American Railway Union. The Association announced that anyone refusing to run Pullman cars would be fired. 5,000 railroad men quit on June 27 and within several days, 125,000 were out and twenty railroads had come to a standstill. The Illinois Governor, who favored labor, refused to call in the state militia. But the U.S. attorney general was a former lawyer for the railroad, and he convinced President Grover Cleveland to send in federal troops because the U.S. mail was not getting through. On July 2, the federal court issued an injunction under the *Sherman Antitrust Act* of 1890 to stop boycotts. Thus, strikers were judged law-breakers, their leaders "engaged in conspiracy to restrain interstate commerce," and federal troops were sent to Chicago.

Both boycott and strike failed and, on July 11, the trains were rolling again. Workers who had not been blacklisted returned to work at their old wages, after signing yellow-dog contracts. The Pullman Strike marked the first incidence of strikebreaking by federal court injunction and showed workers that government supported management. An American president had assumed a new role during a period of national crisis and had used the power of his office to intervene in a dispute between workers and their employers. By 1897, the American Railway Union had folded.

Trust-Busters

I speak of the existence of trusts, combinations and monopolies while the citizen is struggling far in the rear or is trampled to death beneath an iron heel.

— President Grover Cleveland's Message to Congress,
December, 1888

More and more wealth belonged to fewer men, known as "Captains of Industry." Iron and steel, mining, railroads and textile businesses had formed into huge monopolies called trusts. In 1890, Congress passed the *Sherman AntiTrust Act*, meant to curb these giant corporations that dominated America. This act prohibited a corporation merger simply to cut competition by other companies, yet it applied only to corporations involved in interstate business. It also allowed judges to issue *court injunctions*, soon used to smash strikes because managers could simply claim that unions were "corporations of workers who were interrupting trade." Most managers believed government had no business interfering with business anyway.

In 1893, America suffered the worst economic depression of the nineteenth century and with over four million unemployed, the gap between rich and poor grew ever wider. A group of Midwestern farmers, laborers and tradesmen founded the Populist Party. Included in its platform was equality of the races and sexes and its aim was to take control of big business.

Strikes took place all over the country at the turn-of-the-century since Progressives believed society could be transformed if people joined together for social change. The Progressive Movement had a great impact upon social reform and improvements in health and housing. Because it gave ordinary workers confidence to change their conditions, union membership grew. The movement made an impression on Theodore Roosevelt who, as New York City Police Commissioner, visited factories with writer-photographer Jacob Riis, and interviewed young women working in the needle-trades.

Samuel Gompers once asked Roosevelt to support a bill outlawing the making of cigars at home. At first, Roosevelt refused because he thought government should not interfere with business. Gompers then took TR on a tour through crowded tenements where whole families worked day and night, making cigars by hand.

"As a matter of practical common sense I could not vote for continuation of those conditions which I saw," Roosevelt said.

TR Takes Charge

If I were a factory employee, a workman on the railroads, or a wage-earner of any sort, I would undoubtedly join the union of my trade. If I disapproved of its policy, I would join in order to fight that policy; if the union leaders were dishonest, I would join in order to put them out.

— Theodore Roosevelt

The 1902 coal strike set a precedent in labor history because the federal government assumed the role of peacemaker rather than strikebreaker. Theodore Roosevelt became the first president to intervene directly to settle a dispute between labor and management, although he was criticized and even threatened with impeachment for acting as arbitrator.

...I have often been asked what was the most important single event in the labor movement in the United States, and I have invariably replied: the strike of the anthracite coal miners in Pennsylvania.

— Samuel Gompers

Some 150,000 miners, mostly recent immigrants from Eastern Europe, went on strike for shorter hours, higher wages and to gain recognition of the United Mine Workers' Union. The managers refused to meet with workers. George Baer, president of the Philadelphia & Reading Railroad, and a mine owner said, "These men don't suffer. They can't even speak English!"

The mine owners urged President Roosevelt to "do his duty by breaking the strike" and TR visited the coal fields himself.

The acute suffering and scarcity of coal led me to intervene....The urgency of this catastrophe impending over a large portion of our people in the shape of a winter fuel impels me to use personal influence to end a situation which has become literally intolerable ....National Government represents the interest of the public as a whole....Besides labor and management, there is a third party, the great public, with its vital interests and overshadowing rights.

— President Theodore Roosevelt, 1902

The President summoned opposing parties to the White House and established the Anthracite Coal Strike Commission. A compromise was finally reached: a ten percent wage increase instead of the twenty percent requested, a nine hour workday, and labor representatives in the mines to assure fair weighing of coal.

In 1903, Roosevelt established a new government office of Commerce and Labor and appointed its first secretary.

Out of the Sweatshops

The Cost of a $5 Dress

by Frances Perkins (1880-1965)

Frances Perkins was the first woman ever appointed to a U.S. cabinet post. She was director of the New York State Industrial Commission when Franklin Delano Roosevelt was the governor of that state. When he became president in 1933, he named her Secretary of Labor and she held that position until 1945. Her thoughts on work conditions in the sweatshops follow:

Source: *Survey Graphic*, February, 1933, by Leon Stein; reprinted in *Out of the Sweatshop: The Struggle for Industrial Democracy*. International Ladies Garment Workers' Union, AFL-CIO, *New York Times*: Quadrangle Books, Inc. 1977, pp. 224-26.

It hangs in the window of one of the little cash-and-carry stores that now line a street where fashionable New Yorkers used to drive out in their carriages to shop....It is a "supper dress" of silk crepe in the "new red," with medieval sleeves and graceful skirt. A cardboard tag on the shoulder reads: "Special $4.95." Bargain basements and little ready-to-wear shops are filled with "specials."

But the manufacturer who pays a living wage for a reasonable week's work under decent conditions cannot turn out attractive silk frocks to retail at $5 or less. The real cost is borne by the workers in the sweatshops that are springing up in hard-pressed communities. Under today's desperate need for work and wages, girls and women are found toiling overtime at power machines and worktables, some of them for paychecks that represent a wage of less than 10 cents a day.

The sweatshop employer is offending against industry's standards, as well as against the standards of the community. The employer who, in order to pay fair wages for reasonable hours of work, produces dresses in his shop to retail at $9.50, finds himself in competition with the less conscientious manufacturer whose "sweated" garments are offered at $4.95.

This sweatshop proprietor is doing business on a shoestring. He must make a quick turnover or go under. Since he cannot hope to meet union conditions or the requirements of the labor law, he goes to some outlying suburb where garment factories are not a feature of the local picture and where state inspectors are not on the lookout for him. Or perhaps he goes to a nearby state, where labor laws are less stringent or he will escape attention....His work force is made up of wives and daughters of local wage earners who have been out of work for months or even years and whose family situation is desperate. The boss sets the wage rates, figures the pay slips, determines the hours of work. His reply to any complaint is "Quit if you don't like it!"

When Workers Were "Sweaters"

For workers in the garment industry known as "sweaters," the invention of the sewing machine was no labor-saving device, but a symbol of abusive working conditions. Unskilled immigrants, particularly from Russia and Italy, poured into America at the turn-of-the-century, eager for any job. Before the garment industry was unionized, whole families engaged in homework: sewing clothing in tenement rooms rented from their employers. Paid by the piece, they had to provide their own needles, scissors, and thread, and pay rental fees for using the sewing machines. The young women who worked in the "sweatshops" were only slightly better off.

Excerpts from two seamstresses' accounts follow:

Source: Sadie Frowne, *The Independent*, September 25, 1902, from Leon Stein, *ibid.*, pp 60-61.

My name is Sadie Frowne. I work in Allen Street in what they call a sweat-shop. I am new at the work and the foreman scolds me a great deal. I get up at half-past five every morning and make myself a cup of coffee on the oil stove. I eat a bit of bread and perhaps some fruit and then go to work. Often I get there soon after six o'clock so as to be in good time, though the factory does not open till seven.

At seven o'clock we all sit down to our machines and the boss brings to each one the pile of work that he or she is to finish during the day-what they call in English their "stint." This pile is put down beside the machine and as soon as a garment is done it is laid on the other side of the machine. Sometimes the work is not all finished by six o'clock, and then the one who is behind must work overtime.

The machines go like mad all day because the faster you work the more money you get. Sometimes in my haste I get my finger caught and the needle goes right through it. It goes so quick, though, that it does not hurt much. I bind the finger up with a piece of cotton and go on working. We all have accidents like that.

All the time we are working the boss walks around examining the finished garments and making us do them over again if they are not just right. So we have to be careful as well as swift. But I am getting so good at the work that within a year I will be making $7 a week, and then I can save at least $4.50 a week. I have over $200 saved now.

The machines are all run by foot power, and at the end of the day one feels so weak that there is a great temptation to lie right down and sleep. But you must go out and get air and have some pleasure. So instead of lying down I go out, generally with Henry.

Clara Lemlich made labor history when she called for the shirtwaist makers to strike at Cooper Union on November 22, 1909.

Source: *New York Evening Journal*, November 28, 1909.

...The bosses in the shops are hardly what you would call educated men, and the girls to them are part of the machines they are running. They yell at the girls and they call them down even worse than I imagine the Negroes slaves were in the South.

The shops are unsanitary-that's the word that is generally used, but there ought to be a worse one. Whenever we tear or damage any of the goods we sew on, or whenever it is found damaged after we are through with it, whether we have done it or not, we are charged for the piece and sometimes for a whole yard of the material. At the beginning of every slow season, $2 is deducted from our salaries. We have never been able to find out what this is for.

Uprising of the 20,000

Source: *Everybody Sings*, New York: International Ladies Garment Union, May, 1942, p. 23, quoted in Barbara Mayer Wertheimer. *We Were There: The Story of the Working Women in America.* New York: Pantheon, 1977, p. 309.

In the black of the winter of nineteen-nine
When we froze and bled on the picket line,
We showed the world that women could fight,
And we rose and won with women's might.
Hail the waist makers of nineteen-nine,
Making their stand on the picket line,
Breaking the power of those who reign,
Pointing the way, smashing the chain.
And we gave new courage to the men
Who carried on in nineteen-ten
And shoulder to shoulder we'll win through,
Led by ILGWU.

Source: "The First Shirtwaist Walkout," *The Survey*, Dec. 18, 1909.

The fuse that sparked the Uprising of the 20,000 was lighted 18 months before at Triangle Shirtwaist Company when a subcontractor told the manager he "wanted to leave and take the girls with him because he was sick of slave-driving." He was told to pick up his pay and get out immediately, without speaking to any employees. Then he was dragged outside and beaten. "Will you stay at your machines and see a fellow worker treated this way?" he called to the seamstresses. Hearing that, 400 girls shut off their sewing machines and walked out.

On November 22, 1909, at Cooper Union, a meeting was held to express support for strikers and decide upon further action. Samuel Gompers came to offer AF of L support:

Source: Gompers, Nov. 22, 1909, quoted in Leon Stein, *op. cit.*, pp. 69-70.

Yes, Mr. Shirtwaist Manufacturer, it may be inconvenient for you if your boys and girls go out on strike, but there are things of more importance than your convenience and your profit. There are the lives of all the boys and girls working in your business.

If you had an organization before this, it would have stood as a challenge to employers who sought to impose such conditions as you bear. This is the time and the opportunity, and I doubt if you let it pass whether it can be created again in five or ten years or a generation.

I say, friends, do not enter too hastily but when you can't get the manufacturers to give you what you want, then strike. And when you strike, let the manufacturers know you are on strike. Be cool, collected, and determined! Union and progress — let your watchwords be!

After what must have seemed endless speeches by recognized labor leaders, a teenager named Clara Lemlich stood up and requested permission to speak. Many recognized this immigrant worker as the same girl whose ribs had been broken during a recent police charge on the picket line. She addressed the crowd in Yiddish:

Source: Eleanor Flexner, *Century of Struggle: The Woman's Rights Movement in the U.S.*, Cambridge, MA: Harvard University Press, 1968, p. 241.

I am a working girl, and one of those who are on strike against intolerable conditions. I am tired of listening to speakers who talk in general terms. What we are here for is to decide whether or not we shall strike. I offer a resolution that a general strike be declared now!

"The Great Uprising" had begun. For the next several months, until the strike ended on February 15, 1910, many thousands of workers, the majority of them young women between the ages of sixteen and eighteen, walked the picket lines each day through the bitter cold of winter. Many carried banners that read: *We are starving where we work. We might as well starve while we strike!* Each day, hundreds were bullied, clubbed and beaten, arrested, and fined.

Rules for Pickets

Source: Leon Stein, *op. cit.*, p. 72.

- Don't walk in groups of more than two or three.
- Don't stand in front of the shop; walk up and down.
- Don't stop the person you wish to talk to; walk alongside of him.
- Don't get excited and shout when you are talking.
- Don't put your hand on the person you are speaking to. Don't touch his sleeve or button. This may be construed as "technical assault."
- Don't call anyone "scab" or use abusive language of any kind.
- Plead, persuade, appeal, but do not threaten.
- If a policeman arrests you and you are sure that you have committed no offense, take down his number and give it to your Union officers.

Wealthy women, dedicated to social reform, sympathized with the Shirtwaist Makers and set up food kitchens and relief stations for strikers and directed fund-raising efforts and publicity campaigns to describe the plight of the workers. Nicknamed the "Mink Brigade," many were already active in the Women's Trade Union League, founded in 1903, and dedicated to the "eight hour day and a living wage to protect the home." The WTUL put up bail and paid legal fees for jailed strikers. Some members even joined picket lines and went to jail with the strikers.

After World War I, WTUL helped sponsor the Congress for Trade Union Women and establish the International Congress of Working Women, setting up an International Labor Office at the League of Nations. This Congress was later affiliated with the International Federation of Trade Unions, founded in 1901 and continued until 1945. The WTUL disbanded in 1947.

By mid-December of 1909, some three hundred shops had settled, agreeing to workers' demands for a shorter hour week, with no punishments for striking, small wage increases with overtime pay, four holidays a year, with costs of needles and rental of machines to be paid by employers. Some bosses even agreed to a closed shop, where only union members would be hired. As a result, many strikers returned to their sewing machines. When larger firms held out against employees' demands, hundreds continued marching daily, even through snow more than a foot deep.

The Shirtwaist Makers' Strike was the first large-scale strike initiated by women and gave semi-skilled and unskilled immigrant workers a new voice. By taking direct action, these young women had halted a powerful industry for over thirteen weeks and made a lasting impact upon American labor history.

Thousands soon joined the International Ladies Garment Workers (ILGWU), the first permanent union of working women.

Tragedy at Triangle

After the Shirtwaist Makers' Strike, the Triangle Company took many former workers back, yet still required a 59-hour work week and refused to recognize the union. "Our workers can belong if they wish, but we will not deal with union leaders...."

Source: Joan Dash, *We Shall Not be Moved: The Women's Factory Strike of 1909.* New York: Scholastic, Inc., 1996, p. 141.

"My building is fireproof," said Joseph Ashe. "It has a metal fire escape and emergency stairs." The Triangle Shirtwaist Company occupied the top three floors of the 10-story Ashe Building near Washington Square in New York City. It employed a thousand young women, most between the ages of 16 and 24. Half reported for work on Saturday, March 25, 1911, to catch up on backorders which had accumulated during the recent strike. By 4:30 p.m., when someone on the street below first noticed smoke pouring from the top of the building, most of the seamstresses had received their pay envelopes and were shutting down their machines to go home.

The building had no sprinkler system and the one fire escape that Mr. Ashe had bragged about, ended five feet above the ground. As the workers tried desperately to escape, they found the doors locked — a common practice of managers who suspected their employees of stealing bits of lace and ribbon. The sole exit which they passed through for daily inspection to and from work was also locked. The fire engines arrived quickly, but the ladders reached only as far as the seventh floor and the impact of the bodies broke through their nets. As flames engulfed the 8th floor, some fifty workers chose to jump from windows to the sidewalk below, rather than be burned.

One reporter said that he looked upon the bodies on the sidewalk and "remembered their great strike of last year in which these same girls had demanded more sanitary conditions and more safety precautions in the shops. Their dead bodies were the answer."

ILGWU locals immediately organized a relief campaign to assist families whose wage earners were now dead, and contributions poured in. Andrew Carnegie sent $5000. The Women's Trade Union League launched an investigation into conditions in New York factories. Why had the doors been locked? Why were pieces of fabric and oil-soaked rags left on factory floors? Thousands gathered at the Metropolitan Opera House for a memorial service and to hear speeches calling for safety measures and workman's compensation laws.

Not in Vain

Frances Perkins had been an eyewitness at the Triangle Shirtwaist Company fire. She later said that this experience made her determined to spend her life fighting conditions that had allowed such a tragedy to occur. Perkins served on the Factory Investigating Commission organized after the disaster.

Source: "Address at 50th Anniversary Memorial, March 25, 1961," from *The Triangle Fire*, by Leon Stein, *op. cit.*, pp. 200-201.

...Out of that terrible episode came a self-examination of stricken conscience in which the people of this state saw for the first time the individual worth and value of each of those 146 people who fell or were burned in that great fire. And we saw too, the great human value of every individual who was injured in an accident by a machine.

There was a stricken conscience of public guilt and we all felt that we had been wrong, that something was wrong with that building which we had accepted or the tragedy never would have happened. Moved by this sense of stricken guilt, we banded ourselves together to find a way by law to prevent this kind of disaster.

And so it was that the Factory Commission that sprang out of the ashes of the tragedy made an investigation that took four years of searching, of public hearings, of legislative formulations, of pressuring through the legislature the greatest battery of bills to prevent disasters and hardships affecting working people, of passing laws the likes of which have never been seen in any four sessions of any state legislature.

It was the beginning of a new and important drive to bring the humanities to the life of the brothers and sisters we all had in the

36

working groups of these United States. The stirring up of the public conscience and the act of the people in penitence brought about not only these laws; it was also that stirring of conscience which brought about in 1932 the introduction of a new element into the life of the whole United States.

We had in the election of Franklin Roosevelt the beginning of what has come to be called a New Deal for the U. S. ...But it was based really upon the experience that we had in New York and upon the sacrifices of those who, we faithfully remember with affection and respect, died in that terrible fire on March 25, 1911. They did not die in vain....

Frances Perkins, Secretary of Labor, was the first woman cabinet member. She is shown here with Eleanor Roosevelt in 1934. (CONSTITUTION, *Spring/Summer1990 Vol.2 No.2, page 16)*

Bread and Roses

This poem by James Oppenheim (1882-1932) was inspired by banners carried by workers as they marched in picket lines during the Lawrence Textile Strike of 1912. "We want bread and roses too!" not only became a cry for food and decent wages, but also an expression of the need for beauty and dignity in the lives of all working people. The verses which follow, based on the cry of the strikers, first appeared in the April 27, 1946 edition of *Industrial Solidarity*.

As we come marching, marching in the beauty of the day,
A million darkened kitchens, a thousand mill lofts gray,
Are touched with all the radiance that a sudden sun discloses,
For the people hear us singing, "Bread and Roses! Bread and Roses!"

As we come marching, marching we battle too for men,
For they are women's children, and we mother them again.
Our lives shall not be sweated from birth until life closes;
Hearts starve as well as bodies; give us bread, but give us roses!
As we come marching, marching, unnumbered women dead
Go crying through our singing their ancient cry for bread.
Small art and love and beauty their drudging spirits knew.
Yes, it is bread we fight for — but we fight for roses, too!

As we come marching, marching, we bring the greater days.
The rising of the woman means the rising of the race.
No more the drudge and idler — ten that toil while one reposes,
But a sharing of life's glories: Bread and Roses! Bread and Roses!

Library of Congress

Some strikers' children sent to New York to stay in the homes of other workers

The Lawrence Textile Strike

Source: William Cahn, *Lawrence 1912: The Bread & Roses Strike.* N.Y.: Pilgrim Press, 1980 (Reprinted from Mill Town, 1954).

The 1912 Strike at Lawrence, Massachusetts was nicknamed "the singing strike" because textile workers from many countries who spoke different languages sang the same songs as they marched together in picket lines.

"This was a new kind of strike. There had never been any mass picketing in any New England town. Ten thousand workers picketed. It was the spirit of the strikers that seemed dangerous. They were confident...they sang. They were always marching and singing," wrote labor journalist Mary Heaton Vorse.

Cahn goes on to quote *Colliers Magazine.*

The Lawrence Textile Strike was led by the Industrial Workers of the World, IWW, a militant union known as the *Wobblies*, which had been founded at Chicago in 1905 as a response to the exclusion of unskilled workers by the American Federation of Labor. The IWW's dream was to replace capitalism with a socialist system in which workers would own and run industry and enjoy the profits of their labor. "It is wrong to charge that the doctrine of the IWW, as it was preached at Lawrence, was fundamentally a doctrine of violence; fundamentally, it was a doctrine of the brotherhood of man."

Although the IWW directed other successful strikes like the one at Lawrence, membership dwindled and the organization lost prestige when it refused to back America's entry into World War I.

Recollections of a Young Worker

Fred Beal was fifteen and working in the Pacific Mills at the time of the Lawrence Strike. He later became a union organizer for the IWW. This is an excerpt from his personal account of how the strike started.

Source: Fred Beal, *Proletarian Journey*, New York, 1937; from *Civil Liberties in American History*, Da Capo Press Reprint Series, 1971, pp. 32-33; 44.

One day, at noon-time, a lecturer addressed the crowd in front of our mill gate....He urged us to organize into a union, to join the Industrial Workers of the World, and to demand from the bosses more wages and shorter hours. He declared that we textile workers were wage slaves and that all the mill owners were slave drivers...who were enjoying the Florida sunshine while we slaved in the mills for their profit....The Irish workers did not like the speaker; the Italians did. The Irish cupped their hands to their mouths, made noises every time the Italians applauded and yelled: "Ef ye don't like this country, go back where ye come from!"

The speaker ignored these remarks and continued, "The working class and the employing class have nothing in common. Between these two classes a struggle must go on until the workers of the world organize, take possession of the earth and the machinery of production and abolish the wage system."

Then as if by prearrangement, the ten-minutes-to-one bells, high up in the mill's belfry, began tolling their dismal warning to us workers that it was time for us to get back to work. "The slave bells are calling!" yelled the IWW speaker. "The masters want you back at the bench and machine. Go, slaves! But remember, these bells will some day toll the death-knell of the slave drivers!"

That afternoon we talked about the IWW speaker and the union he was organizing. We had good reason to talk. Things were about to happen. The State Legislature had just passed a law reducing the hours of labor from 56 to 54 per week, and there was rumor that our pay would be reduced accordingly. Our next pay day was Friday, January 12, and the grown-up workers were talking about going on strike if wages were cut. We young people thought it would be fun to strike and made plans to go skating and sleigh-riding...all but little Eva. She and her mother were the breadwinners of the family. Her father had lost an arm in Pingree's Box Shop two weeks after they came from Canada. They sorely needed Little Eva's weekly wage of five dollars and four cents.

On this Friday morning the atmosphere at the mill was tense with suppressed excitement. We were not sure the company would cut our wages. We would know when the paymaster came around at eleven o'clock. The shop was full of rumors. One of these was that the big Wood Mill of eight thousand workers had already gone on strike. This almost started an immediate walk-out in our spinning room. Dwyer had it on "good authority" that we would get an increase if we stayed at work. Queenie said the priest had told her not to strike.

Paddy Parker, petition in hand, called me to one side. "Young man, I see your name heads this list. Did you put it there?"

"Yes, I did, because I don't think we should get a wage cut."

"You shouldn't have your name with these foreigners."

"I work with them, don't I?"

"Yes, but we want to get a better position soon, don't you? Stand by the company and I'll cross off your name."

"I'm going on strike if the others do," I said firmly.

"All right, young man, if you do, you will never get work again in the Pacific Mills, and I will see to it that you are blacklisted at other mills, with every other name on this list."

The threat of not being able to get work again in any of the mills made me feel miserable. Where else could I get a job? All Lawrence to me was mills, mills, mills. Perhaps the best thing would be to leave Lawrence and go West, to be a cowboy like those in the movies. For the first time in my life I felt fear tugging at my heart. Hadn't I promised to help out the family? And now, if I went out on strike, I would never get another job in the mills of Lawrence and perhaps Paddy Parker could stop me from getting a job anywhere. I had to make a decision in thirty minutes before the paymaster came around.

There was a sharp whistle. It was the call that said: "Come and get your pay!"

Just like any other Friday, the paymaster, with the usual armed guard, wheeled a cart containing hundreds of pay envelopes to the head of a long line of anxiously waiting people. There was much chattering in different languages....When the great moment came, the first ones nervously opened their envelopes and found that the company had deducted two hours pay. They looked...uncertain what to do. Milling around, they waited for someone to start something. They didn't have long to wait, for one lively young Italian had his mind thoroughly made up and swung into action without even looking into his pay envelope.

"Strike! Strike!" he yelled. To lend strength to his words, he threw his hands in the air like a cheerleader. "Strike! Strike! Strike!" ...A Syrian worker pulled a switch and the powerful speed belts that gave life to the bobbins slackened to a stop. There were cries, "All out!"

Elizabeth Gurley Flynn: The Rebel Girl

Raised in a socialist household in Concord, NH, Elizabeth Gurley Flynn (1890-1975) proudly wore the nickname "The Rebel Girl," given her by *Wobbly* troubadour Joe Hill. Flynn had a busy and brilliant career as a political activist, travelling across the country as a labor organizer for the IWW and directing relief programs for families of strikers. When Gurley, as she was known, was twenty-one, she was sent to Lawrence by the IWW to assist the strikers.

Excerpts from her personal account follow:

Source:Elizabeth Gurley Flynn, *The Rebel Girl: My First Life (1906-1926)*, New York: International Publishers, 1955; 1976, Chapter Three.

...The small pittance taken from the workers by the rich corporations...was the spark that ignited the general strike. "Better to starve fighting than to starve working!" became their battle-cry. It spread from mill to mill. In a few hours of that cold, snowy day, 14,000 workers poured out of the mills. In a few days the mills were empty and still — and remained so for nearly three months.

...It was estimated that there were at least 25 different nationalities in Lawrence. The largest groups among the strikers were: Italians, 7,000; Germans, 6,000; French Canadians, 5,000; all English speaking, 5,000; Poles, 2,500; Lithuanians, 2,000; Franco-Belgians, 1,100; Syrians, 1,000 — with a sprinkling of Russians, Jews, Greeks, Letts and Turks. The local IWW became the organizing core of the strike. They were overwhelmed by the magnitude of the job they had on their hands and sent a telegram for help to Ettor in New York City. He and his friend, Arturo Giovannitti, responded to the call on the promise of Haywood, myself and others to come as soon as possible....

Ettor selected interpreters to bring order out of this tower of Babel. They organized mass meetings in various localities of the different language groups and had them elect a strike committee of men and women which represented every mill, every department and every nationality. They held meetings of all the strikers together on the Lawrence Common so that the workers could realize their oneness and strength.

Haywood came to Lawrence on January 21, 1912 and was greeted at the railroad station by 15,000 strikers, who escorted him to the Common....There were 1,400 state militiamen in Lawrence, which was like an armed camp. Clashes occurred daily between the strikers and the police and state troopers....

Wherever Bill Haywood went, the workers followed him with glad greetings. They roared with laughter and applause when he said, "The AFL organizes like this!" — separating his fingers as far apart as they would go and naming them — "Weavers, loom-fixers, dyers, spinners." Then he would say: "The IWW organizes like this!" — tightly clenching his big fist, shaking it at the bosses....

...We held special meetings for the women at which Haywood and I spoke. The women worked in the mills for lower pay and in addition had all the housework and care of the children. The old-world attitude of man as the "lord and master" was strong. At the end of the day's work — or now, on strike duty — the man went home and sat at ease while his wife did all the work preparing the meal, cleaning the house, etc. There was considerable male opposition to women going to meetings and marching on the picket line. We resolutely set out to combat these notions. The women wanted to picket. They were strikers as well as wives and were valiant fighters....

Suffering increased among the strikers....A proposal was made by some of the strikers that we send the children out of Lawrence to be cared for in other cities. On February 17, 1912, the first group of 150 children were taken to New York City....Five thousand people met them at Grand Central Station. People wept when they saw the poor clothes and thin shoes of these wide-eyed little children....

On February 24, a group of 40 strikers' children were to go from Lawrence to Philadelphia....At the railroad station, where the children were assembled accompanied by their fathers and mothers, just as they were ready to board the train they were surrounded by police. Troopers surrounded the station outside to keep others out. Children were clubbed and torn away from their parents and a wild scene of brutal disorder took place. Thirty-five frantic women and children were arrested, thrown screaming and fighting into patrol wagons. They were beaten into submission and taken to the police station. There the women were charged with "neglect" and improper guardianship and ten frightened children were taken to the Lawrence Poor Farm. The police station was besieged by enraged strikers. Members of the Philadelphia Committee were arrested and fined. It was a day without parallel in American labor history. A reign of terror prevailed in Lawrence, which literally shook

America....Samuel Gompers denounced the action of the police as "a crime...."

The House Rules Committee held a hearing in Washington, D. C. in March of 1912...16 children went to Washington to testify. All of these children were strikers. A 16 year old boy testified that he worked for the American Woolen Company for $5.10 a week. A 15 year old testified that he liked to go to school and got as far as the seventh grade. "Why did you leave?" a Congressman asked. "Well, we had to have bread and it was hard to get," the child answered....

On March 1, 1912, the American Woolen Company announced a 7.5 % increase in 33 cities. On March 6, 125,000 workers in cotton and woolen mills of six states were raised 5 to 7 per cent. On March 14, the Lawrence strike was settled with the American Woolen Company, the Atlantic Mill and other mills. Twenty thousand workers assembled on the Common to hear the report....The demands which they had won secured an increase in wages from 5 to 20%; increased compensation for overtime...and no discrimination against any worker who had taken part in the strike.

"Labor has seldom, if ever, won so complete a victory," Lincoln Steffens wrote in the *New York Globe.* "The Lawrence Textile Strike is a clear cut triumph for the workers." (*Literary Digest*, March 23, 1912.) The Lawrence Strike became a model for workers' solidarity and non-violent passive resistance. "Few strikes involving so large a number of employees have continued with so little actual violence or riot," commented the U. S. Department of Labor. National attention had been focused on the living and working conditions of the men, women and children employed in American factories. The Lawrence strike lasted nine and a half weeks, but its impact would be felt for years to come. This strike also showed workers and managers the power that labor united could have.

Birth of the Department of Labor

President William Howard Taft actually signed the bill to create the U. S. Department of Labor just before he left office. The department's establishment early in Woodrow Wilson's administration marked a great achievement for organized labor. From 1865 through 1913, over one hundred bills and resolutions had been presented to Congress for the creation of an agency for labor within the federal government. In 1884, there had been an ineffectual Bureau of Labor under the Department of the Interior. Now, William B. Wilson, a former coal miner and a founder of the United Mine Workers, active in the 1902 coal strikes, was appointed the nation's first Secretary of Labor.

> The great guiding purpose of the Department of Labor is to foster, promote, and develop the welfare of the wage earners of the United States by improving their working conditions and advancing their opportunities for profitable employment....Nor is there any implication that the wage earners in whose behalf this Department was created consist of such only as are associated together in labor unions. It was created in the interests of the welfare of all wage earners of the United States, whether organized or unorganized....The element of fairness to every interest is of equal importance, and the Department has had fairness between wage earner and wage earner, between wage earner and employer, between employer and employer, and between each and the public as a whole the supreme motive and purpose of its activities...through realization of the highest ideals of industrial justice.
>
> — President Woodrow Wilson,
> on establishment of Labor Cabinet Post, March 4, 1913

Labor made great advances under President Wilson. For the first time in American history labor leaders participated in forming government policy. Labor sat down with government and business on the Railroad Wage Commission, the National War Labor Board, and the President's Mediation Commission. The National War Labor Board settled disputes by mediation and acknowledged the right of collective bargaining and union recognition. In turn, unions pledged not to strike and wage disputes were settled by boards. If business refused to abide by board decisions, government could seize and operate the industry, which happened with the railroads.

The 54-hour week became law. Railroad workers got the eight-hour workday, paving the way for other industries. The Factory Safety Law and Child Labor Law were passed in 1913. The U. S. Employment Service was established and hourly wages rose. Union membership doubled during Wilson's presidency.

The Clayton Act

The AF of L pressured Congress to pass the Clayton Act to update the Sherman Act of 1890. The Clayton bill exempted labor from prosecution under the Sherman Act and limited the rights of courts to issue injunctions. Samuel Gompers called it "Labor's Magna Carta."

According to the Clayton Act, passed by Congress October 15, 1914, "the labor of a human being is not considered a commodity or article of commerce." Nor could labor unions be considered "illegal combinations or conspiracies in restraint of trade," meaning that strikes, picketing, and boycotts were now legal. Court injunctions restraining labor could be used only to prevent injury to property.

Pittsburgh Chronicle Telegraph, October, 1919

The strike called on September 22, 1919 was a battle between America's most powerful industrial company, the United States Steel Corporation, and 300,000 workers in eight states. A national labor committee representing twenty-four AF of L unions recruited steelworkers into the Amalgamated Association of Iron, Steel and Tin Workers.

By January, 1920, labor admitted defeat and steelworkers returned to the mills without winning any demands. Unions would not gain a foothold in the steel plants for another generation.

The New Deal — Labor's Golden Years

"Our greatest primary task is to put people to work," Franklin Delano Roosevelt announced at his first inaugural address in March of 1933. To counteract the Great Depression, Congress had already passed the *Norris-LaGuardia Act* the preceding year, affirming labor's right to organize without interference from employers. It also outlawed unfair labor practices such as yellow-dog contracts, and prohibited federal courts from issuing injunctions during most labor disputes.

"Uncle Sam Protects You! You Can't Be Fired For Joining The Union!" were signs of the times during FDR's administration, when labor's position was strengthened by new federal laws, spearheaded by U. S. Secretary of Labor, Frances Perkins.

> The isolated worker today is a mere connection link in an impersonalized and heartless machine. He is powerless to defend himself....Effective contact between the two [worker and industry] is physically impossible. That is why the right to bargain collectively is necessary not only to social justice for the worker, but equally to the wise and rational conduct of business affairs.
>
> — Senator Robert F. Wagner
> Address to U. S. Senate, 1935

The National Labor Relations Act, known as the Wagner Act, and signed by President Roosevelt on July 5, 1935, was a landmark for the American labor movement. Incorporating language previously adopted in Section 7(a) of the National Industrial Recovery Act, 1933, it guaranteed employees the "right to self-organization, to form, join or assist labor organizations to bargain collectively through representatives of their own choosing, and to engage in concerted activities for the purpose of collective bargaining or other mutual aid or protection."

A National Labor Relations Board representing labor and management interests was set up to prevent unfair labor practices, hear grievances, and settle disputes. This federal board also supervised elections when workers voted for or against having a union in their plants. In April of 1937, the controversial Wagner Act was upheld and strengthened by a Supreme Court ruling that declared workers were entitled to the same rights as employers.

The Fair Labor Standards Act was passed by Congress on June 25, 1938 to establish maximum hours in the work week and a minimum wage. A

FLASH!! FLASH!!

As this bulletin goes to press, word has just been received that the Wagner Labor Disputes Bill, outlawing company unions, has just been passed by Congress. This bill, even more than the N. R. A., insures the workers' right to collective bargaining.   Come to the meeting Sunday, and find out what this will mean to you.

UNION MEETING

Sunday, June 23, – 1 p. m.

at Polish Falcon Hall, 4130 Junction

TO ALL KELSEY-HAYES EMPLOYEES:

Have you thought about where YOUR Protection was coming from now that the Blue Eagle of N. R. A. is officially dead?

YOU'RE GOING TO NEED PROTECTION—PLENTY!

Already some foremen and would-be big shots are starting their chiseling and cheating. We do not believe this conforms to the managements idea of fair play and square dealing.

YOUR UNION IS YOUR ONLY PROTECTION!

Your Union is in existence solely for Your Protection. Your Union is prepared to protect you

USE IT by reporting any case of chiseling or cheating to Your Union officials. They will take it to the Management where we have been promised a square deal.

SPECIAL NOTICE— You can now join or be reinstated for $1.00. On and after July 1st the bargain prices for reinstatement and initiation will be over. On that date re-instatement will again be $2.40 and the initiation fee $2.00.

ACT NOW -- JOIN YOUR UNION!

Sponsored by the Educational Committee of Federal Labor Union No. 18677, Affiliated with American Federation of Labor.

ROBOTNICY POLSCY!

Czy pomyśliliście nad tem, kto obecnie da Wam opiekę po zniesieniu N. R. A.?   Opieki tej będziecie potrzebować i tylko prawdziwa Unia może Wam dać prawdziwą opiekę. Już teraz niektórzy formani i inni bosowie pozwalają sobie na prześladowania i oszukaństwa. Wasza Unia jest Waszą jedyną obroniciełką. Raportujcie do Unji o każdej Waszej krzywdzie. Urzędnicy Unji dopomogą Wam i upomną się za Wami w zarządzie fabryki.

SPECJALNE ZAWIADOMIENIE!

Obecnie jeszcze możecie skorzystać ze zniżonej opłaty i wstąpić do Unji za $1. Od 1-go lipca wstęp do Unji kosztować będzie $3. Ci, którzy wystąpili z Unji mogą spowrotem wstąpić za opłatą $1. DZIAŁAJCIE NATYCHMIAST — WSTĄPCIE DO UNPI ZARAZ!

Przyjdźcie na Mityng Unijny w Niedzielę, 23-go Czerwca, 1935, o godzinie 1-ej po południu do Sokolni, 4130 Junction Ulica, blisko Buchanan Ulicy.

37

Collective bargaining issues were central to the Wagner Act. Union Meeting Bulletin, June 1935. (From Jackdaw No. A. 33: The CIO & Labor Movement, Exhibit 1) milestone in labor legislation, its purpose was to "eliminate labor conditions detrimental to the maintenance of the minimum standard of living necessary for health, efficiency, and well-being of workers." The Act established a 44-hour week maximum for the first year on the job, 42 hours the second, and 40 hours thereafter. Minimum wage was to be 25 cents an hour the first year, 30 cents the second, and forty cents for the next six years. Federal law now required employers to pay time-and-a-half for overtime. The Fair Labor Standards Act has been amended several times in order to increase the minimum wage.

John L. Lewis: The Miners' Friend

John Llewellyn Lewis (1897-1969) was the son of an immigrant coal miner from Wales who got blacklisted for leading a strike. After attending the first national convention of the United Mine Workers in 1906, Lewis decided to become a union organizer and when the AF of L granted an industrial union charter to UMW two years later, Gompers appointed Lewis a field representative. When a mine accident killed 160, Lewis pressured the Illinois State Legislature to pass safety measures. He became President of the United Mine Workers in 1919 and held that post forty years.

John L. Lewis Organizes the Unorganized!

The thing that gives me strength is the fact that I am able correctly to interpret the aims of my people. I know the psychology of the coal miner. I know about his dreams and his ideals and trials and tribulations. I have lived with coal miners. I am one of them. My family has been associated with the mining industry for a century and a half and an understanding of the miner's problems is inbred in me....I have laid down in a mine tunnel with my face in a half inch of water, and pulled my shirt up over my head, expecting to die the next minute in an explosion....And when God performed a miracle and stopped that explosion before I died, I think it gave me some understanding of what men think about and how they suffer when they are waiting to die in a coal mine explosion.... When I speak, I speak the thoughts of the membership of the United Mine Workers of America, because I understand them....I have never faltered or failed to present the cause or plead the case of the mine workers of this country. I have pleaded your cause from the pulpit and the public platform; in joint conference with the operators of this country; before the bar of state legislatures; in the councils of the President's cabinet; and in the public press of this nation — not in the quavering tones of a feeble mendicant asking alms, but in the thundering voice of the captain of a mighty host, demanding the rights to which free men are entitled.

— John L. Lewis
Excerpt from Speech at Annual Convention
A F of L, 1934

A 1936 cartoon illustrated the split in American labor being pulled in opposite directions by John L. Lewis and William Green.

The failure of the Great Steel Strike of 1919 convinced Lewis that the American labor movement needed to make fundamental changes. The AF of L, made up of skilled workers organized by crafts, did not include the non-skilled labor force of millions involved in mass production, performing their jobs on assembly lines in huge plants that produced automobiles, rubber, and steel. At their convention of October, 1935, Lewis told AF of L members that their organization no longer truly represented the majority of American workers.

On November 9, 1935, the Committee for Industrial Organization was founded within the AF of L. William Green, who had become AF of L president after Gompers' death, was, like Lewis, a former coal miner. Because of the many differences with the new industrial union, the CIO was expelled from the AF of L in 1938, and changed its name to the Congress of Industrial Organizations, with John L. Lewis as president. This new labor organization gained immediate support from millions of workers. No fees were required for membership and the CIO opened its doors to include blacks and women workers. This feud between craft unionists and industrial unionists continued for another twenty years.

Strikers, Sit Down!

Although John L. Lewis and the CIO did not originate the "sit-down strike," it was a tactic he often advised. One sit-down strike started in Atlanta in November of 1936 when four workers got fired for wearing union buttons. There were nine hundred sit-down strikes in the country over the next two years. By remaining inside their factories, workers could not be easily replaced by scabs hired by employers, nor risk physical injury in attacks on the picket lines.

Determined to "organize the unorganized," the CIO targeted the automobile industry. Workers were not unionized at Ford, Chrysler, or General Motors. GM even hired spies to prevent union activities, so that any employee suspected of union membership was fired. Workers at GM plants were even afraid to talk to one another for fear of being accused of labor organizing. In 1936, workers who made rubber tires in Akron, Ohio, staged a sit-down, refusing to leave the plant until wages were increased and management recognized their union, the United Automobile Workers of America, headed by Walter Reuther. At the Fisher Plant in Flint, Michigan and GM plants in six other cities, workers also sat down. When the police tried to storm the factories with teargas, workers held them off with firehoses. Although managers turned off the heat, tried to prevent families from delivering food to the strikers, made an unsuccessful attempt to get a court injunction for "damages against private property," and got the governor to send in troops, strikers finally forced management to come to terms with the CIO/UAW using the same methods of civil disobedience that would prove so effective during the Civil Rights Movement.

Sit Down, Sit Down!

Source: Maurice Sugar, Attorney, UAW, 1937.

When they tie the can to a Union man
Sit down! Sit Down!
When they give him the sack, they'll take him back,
Sit down! Sit Down!

CHORUS;   *Sit Down, just take a seat*
       Sit down and rest your feet
       Sit down, you've got'em beat
       Sit down! Sit Down!

When they smile and say no raise in pay
Sit down! Sit Down!
When you want the boss to come across
Sit down! Sit Down!
When the speed-up comes, just twiddle your thumbs.
Sit down! Sit Down!

When they want'em to know they'd better go slow
Sit down! Sit Down!
When the boss won't talk, don't take a walk.
Sit down! Sit Down!
When the boss sees that, he'll want a little chat.
Sit down! Sit Down!

The Taft-Hartley Act

Source: Report of the Senate Subcommittee on Labor & Public Welfare, April 17, 1947; Bill S. 1126; Submitted by Robert Taft, R/Ohio, in Shwartz-Koretz, "Labor Organization," *Statutory History of the U. S.* New York: McGraw-Hill/Chelsea House, 1970, pp. 555-88.

"Bad for labor. Bad for management. Bad for the country! It will reverse the basic direction of our national labor policy." This is what Harry S. Truman said about the Labor-Management Relations Act, known as the Taft-Hartley Act, which was passed by Congress a second time, over his presidential veto, to become law on June 23, 1947. AF of L president George Meany believed it negated the New Deal's pro-labor legislation and took the labor movement back to the early 1800s when trade unions had no legal right to organize and were considered "criminal conspiracies."

After World War II, as America's economy adapted from war to peacetime production and wages failed to keep up with rising living costs, a series of strikes erupted all over the country in various industries. Union membership grew from five million in 1940 to 15 million by 1945. A "Great Strike Wave" rolled across the country with 4,985 strikes occurring in 1946 alone, in nearly every major industry. Anti-union feelings were running high with the public, even though these strikes had been among the most peaceful in history. Supporters of the Taft-Hartley Act believed labor had abused its power and said that although the National Labor Relations Act had been passed to aid unions, the balance of rights and responsibilities between workers and management was now endangering the national economy. They now considered labor unions disruptive to American production.

Nicknamed the "Slave Labor Law" by opponents, the Taft-Hartley Act amended the National Labor Relations Act "to provide additional facilities for the mediation of labor disputes affecting commerce and to equalize legal responsibilities of labor organizations and employers." This Act:

- banned or limited collective bargaining rights established by the Wagner Act
- banned the closed shop, which prohibited the hiring of non-union men
- permitted union shops only if the majority of workers voted for it; under *right-to-work* laws individual states had the power to outlaw union shops even if they had been voted in by employees

- permitted employers to sue unions for breach of contract or damages inflicted during strikes
- required unions to abide by a 60-day "cooling-off" period before going on strike
- forbade federal employees to strike
- gave government the right to seek court injunctions against workers out on strike more than 80 days, and/or considered a threat to national welfare by stopping work
- required unions to file their constitutions and financial statements with the U. S. Labor Department
- forbade union contributions to political campaigns
- ended the "check-off system" in which the employer collected union dues and regulated union dues
- required union leaders to take an oath and sign affidavits that they were not members of the Communist party
- declared some union tactics, such as boycotts, to be *unfair labor practices*

New Strength in the 20th Century

Labor Finds Strength in Unity — AFL-CIO

The kind of labor movement we want is not committed to a nickel-in-the-pay envelope philosophy. We are building a labor movement, not to patch up the world so men can starve less frequently, but a labor movement that will remake the world so that working people will get the benefit of their labor.

— Walter Reuther, Pres. of CIO and UAW
V.P. of AFL-CIO 1955-68

Organized labor had increasingly worked through political channels to get legislators elected who would work to repeal the Taft-Hartley Act and lobby for labor's interests in Washington. Union membership had fallen drastically, and it was clear that if labor were to maintain any influence in American life, the unions would have to set aside personal rivalries and political differences. Since 1935, there had been two major labor groups in the U. S. which divided skilled and unskilled workers. Now labor came together in mutual purpose following anti-labor legislation like the Taft-Hartley Act. A committee was established from the AF of L and the CIO to draft a constitution for one great organization.

George Meany (1884-1980), a plumber by trade and AFL president beginning in 1952, is chiefly credited with the merger of the American Federation of Labor and the Congress of Industrial Organizations (AFL-CIO) on December 5, 1955, an action that publicly demonstrated labor's united front.

Twelve major aims of AFL-CIO were stated in their new constitution:

- To aid workers in securing better wages, hours, and working conditions with due regard for the autonomy and integrity of affiliated unions.
- To promote the organization of the unorganized into unions of their own choosing, giving recognition to both craft and industrial unionism.
- To encourage formation of locals, state and local central bodies, and nationals, and affiliation of such organizations with the new federation.
- To encourage all workers without regard to race, creed, or national origin to share in the full benefits of unionism.
- To secure legislation safeguarding and promoting the principle of free collective bargaining.
- To protect and strengthen the nation's democratic institutions.
- To promote the cause of peace and freedom throughout the world.
- To preserve and maintain the integrity of each affiliated union in the organization.
- To encourage the sale and use of union-made goods and union services.
- To protect the labor movement from corrupt influences and the undermining effect of communist groups opposed to the basic principles of democracy.
- To safeguard the democratic character of the labor movement.
- To encourage workers to register and vote and exercise their full rights and responsibilities.

Cesar E. Chavez

La Huelga! and the California Grape Boycott

The migratory farm workers who picked crops from the Mexican to the Canadian borders had never really been part of the American labor movement. It was not until 1959 that the AFL-CIO included an Agricultural Workers Organizing Committee. Known as campesinos, these families worked the harvests in season, picking vegetables and grapes in California vineyards. Most were Chicanos or Mexican-Americans, and Filipinos, whose relatives had left the Philippines in the 1920s because they had heard California's Central Valley was the "Land of Opportunity." Instead, they worked for wages so low that they could not adequately feed or clothe their families. Their children had to quit school to go into the fields. Chemical pesticides, used to stimulate growth of the produce, burned their eyes and made them sick. They were housed in crowded dormitories or shacks and were not even supplied with safe drinking water. Determined to change this "feudal system" and improve the lives of migrant workers, Cesar Chavez organized the National Farm Workers' Association.

In 1965, Chavez combined the Agricultural Workers Organizing Committee and National Farm Workers' Association to form a new union, the United Farm Workers of America (UFWA).

The UFWA began an organized protest against the use of chemical pesticides on California grapes. Their campaign was called "La Causa." Their strike lasted five years, the longest national boycott in the history of American labor. Chavez organized La Causa nationally, so all Americans would become aware of the deplorable living and working conditions of families who had picked the grapes for their tables and would no longer buy nonunion products. Cesar Chavez always insisted that La Huelga [the strike] was really about human dignity.

La Causa

Source: Excerpts from a letter of Cesar E. Chavez to E. L. Barr, Jr., President of California Grape & Tree Fruit League, reproduced in George Horwitz, *La Causa: The California Grape Strike.* New York: Macmillan, 1970.

I am sad to hear about your accusations in the press that our union movement and grape boycott have been successful because we have used violence and terror tactics. If what you say is true, I have been a failure and should withdraw from the struggle....We are men and women who have suffered and endured much and not only because of our abject poverty but because we have been kept poor. The colors of our skins, the languages of our cultural and native origins, the lack of formal education, the exclusion from the democratic process, the numbers of our slain in recent wars-all these burdens generation after generation have sought to demoralize us, to break our human spirit. But God knows that we are not beasts of burden, we are not agricultural implements or rented slaves, we are men.

...Time accomplishes for the poor what money does for the rich. ...We advocate militant nonviolence as our means for social revolution and to achieve justice for our people...we have tried to involve masses of people in their own struggle. Participation and self-determination remain the best experience of freedom...we do not hate you or rejoice to see your industry destroyed; we hate the agribusiness system that seeks to keep us enslaved and we shall overcome and change it not by retaliation or bloodshed but by a determined non-violent struggle carried on by those masses of farm workers who intend to be free and human.

The grape boycott made history. By the end of the 1970s, the UFWA had won the right of collective bargaining, higher wages and better living conditions for the California farmworkers. Yet today, fewer than ten percent of U. S. farmworkers belong to unions.

President Kennedy's Tribute to Unions

On May 19, 1962, President John Fitzgerald Kennedy dedicated an International Ladies Garment Workers' Union cooperative housing project in New York City.

Source: Excerpt from JFK's Speech at Dedication of ILGWU Housing Site, *The New York Times*, May 20, 1962, p. 62.

What can a union now do to contribute to the welfare of its own members and to the welfare of the country? One of the great problems you face in organized labor is how to maintain the same fervor, the same spirit, the same zeal which motivated this and other unions in their early days of the great struggle to provide decent working conditions and pay for their members.

We still have great areas of effort which are left to this union in protecting the welfare of its members. But it is also important to emphasize that there is also a great opportunity open to all unions across the country to participate in the strengthening of the country....The work for organized labor in the United States today is just as important, in many ways, more important than it was 25 years ago.

...If you want to have equal opportunity for all Americans, if we want to rebuild our cities, if we want to provide transit in and out of our cities, if we want to educate our children, if we want to have colleges and universities to which they can go, if we want to have medical schools to train our doctors, if we want to make this country as wonderful a place as it can be for the 300,000,000 who will live in this country within 40 years, then we have to do our task today. It is the task of every generation to build a road for the next generation....

Suggested Further Reading

Note: Major sources are cited in each section of the text, and are also recommended for further reading.

Altman, Linda Jacobs. *The Pullman Strike of 1894: Turning Point for American Labor.* Brookfield, CT: Millbrook Press, 1995.

Cobblestone. The History Magazine for Young People. "The History of Labor." Vol. 13, #8, Peterborough, New Hampshire, October, 1992.

Fisher, Leonard Everett. *The Unions.* New York: Holiday House, 1982. (elementary)

Gardner, Joseph L. *Labor on the March: The Story of America's Unions.* New York: Harper & Row, American Heritage Junior Library, 1969.

Kent, Zachary. *The Story of the Triangle Factory Fire.* Chicago, Illinois: Children's Press, 1989. (elementary)

Kornbluh, Joyce, editor. *Rebel Voices: An I. W. W. Anthology.* Ann Arbor, Michigan: University of Michigan Press, 1964.

Lens, Sidney. *Unions and What They Do.* New York: G. P. Putnam's Sons, 1968.

McKissack, Patricia and Frederick. *The Long Hard Journey: The Story of the Pullman Porter.* New York: Walker & Co., 1989.

Madison, Charles A. *American Labor Leaders.* New York: Frederic Ungar, 1962.

Meltzer Milton. *Bread and Roses: The Struggle of American Labor, 1865-1915.* New York: New American Library/Division of Penguin Books; A Mentor Book, 1967.

Naden, Corinne J. *The Haymarket Affair, Chicago 1886: The "Great Anarchist" Riot and Trial.* New York: Franklin Watts, Inc., 1968.

Schwartz, Alvin. *The Unions: What They Are; How They Came to Be; How They Affect Each of Us.* New York: Viking Press, 1972.

Scopino, A. J., Jr., editor. *The Progressive Movement: 1900-1917.* Carlisle, MA: Discovery Enterprises, Ltd. 1996.

Shanker, Albert. Weekly paid columns in *The New York Times,* each Sunday.

Teaching Aids, Songs, and Videos

Songs for Labor: AFL-CIO Publication #56. AFL-CIO Department of Education, Washington, D. C., December, 1983.

Teaching Labor Studies in the Schools, Volumes I & II. Washington, D. C.: International Brotherhood of Teamsters, Dept. of Human Services, 25 Louisiana Ave., NW, 1987, 1988.

"The CIO and the Labor Movement," compiled by Dennis East. Jackdaw A-33 contains copies of historical documents with study notes and reading list. Jackdaw Publications, Division of Golden Owl Publishing, P. O. Box 503, Amawalk, New York 10501-0503 (914)-962-6911.

The American Worker's Story. Lowell Historic Preservation Commission & The Greater Lowell Central Labor Council; Kamber Group, Producer. Narrated by Edward Asner. (16 minutes) 1989. Contact Lowell National Historical Park, Lowell, MA (508)-970-5000 or Tsongas Center for Industrial History, Boott Mill #8, Foot of John St., Lowell, MA 01852

Collective Voices: The Textile Strike of 1912. 20 minutes, with Curriculum Guide. Produced by the Office of the MA Secretary of State, the Massachusetts AFL-CIO and the Commonwealth Museum; Boston, MA, 1990. Contact Commonwealth Museum, 220 Morrissey Blvd., Boston, MA 02125.

About the Editor

Juliet Haines Mofford has been interested in labor history ever since Pete Seeger performed union songs at Oakwood Friends School where she was a student. More recently, as Cultural Director for the Lowell Historic Preservation Commission, Juliet supervised several educational projects on labor history, including a video, *American Workers' Story.* Her article, "Women Wage-earners, 1600s-1940s," appeared in *Women's History Magazine* (March, 1996).

After earning her AB from Tufts University, Juliet attended graduate school at Boston University and in Frankfurt, Germany. She taught in Japan, Spain, and the Caribbean, then worked professionally as a reference librarian. At the Museum of American Textile History, she demonstrated pre-industrial spinning and weaving and operated textile machines like those used in the Lawrence factories at the time of the 1912 strike. As a museum educator, she has specialized in designing museum-to-school curricula and scripting historical plays from original documents.

A freelance writer for over 25 years, Juliet has four books about New England history in print, two of which received national awards. She served as a "stringer" for the *Boston Globe* and *Scholastic Teacher.* Juliet also edited *Cry Witch!: The Salem Witchcraft Trials of 1692* for this *Perspectives on History Series.* She is currently a consultant for Museum Education Services.